Contents

Introduction

If you are wild about learning and wild about animals – this book is for you!

It will take you on a wild adventure, where you will practise key English skills and explore the amazing world of animals along the way.

Each English topic is introduced in a clear and simple way with lots of interesting activities to complete so that you can practise what you have learned.

Alongside every English topic you will uncover fascinating facts about animals of the rainforest. Here, trees are very tall, the weather is warm and there is lots of rain. In some rainforests it rains heavily nearly every day of the year!

When you have completed each topic, record the animals that you have seen and the skills that you have learned in the explorer's logbook on pages 44–45.

Good luck, explorer!

Alison Head

Shh ... silent letters!

As you explore the English language, you will find that some words contain letters you can't hear at all when the word is said out loud.

k̲nuckle   lamb̲   hal̲f

Hundreds of years ago, people would have pronounced these letters. Today we just need to remember to add them when we write the words!

Task 1

Identify and underline the silent letter in each word.

a chalk

b limb

c gnome

d knee

e island

f raspberry

g dumb

h whistle

i comb

j write

k thumb

l write

m knit

n sign

o crumb

p wrist

FACT FILE

Animal: Poison dart frog
Habitat: Tropical rainforests of Central and South America
Weight: 0.2 to 6 g
Lifespan: 3 to 15 years
Diet: Spiders and small insects

WILD FACT

The golden poison dart frog is thought to be the most poisonous vertebrate on earth.

Task 2 Write two words with silent letters for each pair.

a wr_____   wr_____

b _____mb   _____mb

c sc_____   sc_____

d _____lk   _____lk

e _____gn   _____gn

f gh_____   gh_____

Task 3 Underline a spelling mistake in each sentence. Write the correct word in the space.

a A poison dart frog's bright colouring is a warning sine.   _____

b Their predators now that these frogs are dangerous.   _____

c They need to be on their gard around the frogs.   _____

d There is no dout these little frogs are dangerous!   _____

Exploring Further ...

Use the clues to unscramble the anagrams in bold.

a Winter, spring, summer, _____   **TUANUM**

b Quiet, placid. _____   **AMLC**

c The bend in your leg. _____   **ENEK**

d Prickly Scottish flower. _____   **SELHTIT**

Now hop to pages 44–45 to record what you have learned in your explorer's logbook.

Homophones

You will sometimes discover two words that **sound** the same but have a different meaning and spelling. Words like this are called **homophones**.

cereal   serial

It can be very easy to use the wrong word by mistake so you need to look out for these tricky words and check your work carefully.

Task 1 Choose a word on a tropical flower to match each definition.

dessert   aloud   dear

deer   allowed   desert

a dry, sandy region _____

b sweet pudding _____

c permitted _____

d out loud _____

e woodland animal _____

f cherished _____

Task 2
Find the incorrect homophone and underline it in these sentences.

a We began our assent of the mountain at dawn.

b By the middle of the mourning we were feeling exhausted.

c The explorer, who's bag was heaviest, grew very tired.

d Their wasn't much further to go!

WILD FACT

Hummingbirds can hover in mid-air and can fly backwards and upside down.

Task 3
Select the most suitable word to complete each sentence.

a Our journey was made harder by the <u>recent / resent</u> rainfall.

b I <u>lead / led</u> the way, taking care on the slippery path.

c We passed a <u>stationary / stationery</u> vehicle, stuck in the flood.

d We had to <u>proceed / precede</u> with great caution.

Exploring Further ...
Write your own sentences including these easily confused words.

a advice _____

_____

b advised _____

_____

c guest _____

_____

d guessed _____

_____

Now fly to pages 44–45 to record what you have learned in your explorer's logbook.

Tricky word endings

If you listen carefully, you will discover that the word endings **cious** and **tious** both sound the same.

cons<u>cious</u>   supersti<u>tious</u>

You need to take care to use the correct endings when you are spelling words.

Task 1
Underline the correct word in each pair.

a spatious   spacious

b gracious   gratious

c nutritious   nutricious

d vitious   vicious

e facetious   facecious

Task 2
Add c or t to complete each word.

a pre__ious   b cau__ious

c ambi__ious   d deli__ious

e ficti__ious   f lus__ious

g cons__ious

Task 3 Investigating word endings can help to build your vocabulary. Match these less common **tious** and **cious** words with the correct definition.

Word	Definition
a vivacious	really tasty
b malicious	determined
c scrumptious	tiresomely repetitive
d tenacious	lively, energetic
e repetitious	spiteful or intended to harm

WILD FACT

Capybaras are rodents, like rabbits, guinea pigs and mice. They are the world's largest rodent and can weigh as much as a man!

Exploring Further ...

Find the **cious** or **tious** words in the box that match these clues.

ferocious	ostentatious	atrocious
luscious	contentious	suspicious

a disbelieving, wary _____

b savagely fierce _____

c showing off to impress _____

d having a delicious taste or smell _____

e likely to cause disagreement _____

f shockingly bad, cruel or brutal _____

Now splash to pages 44–45 to record what you have learned in your explorer's logbook.

Formal or informal?

When we write, we need to think about who will be reading our work. Expert writers vary what they say and how they say it, depending on their **audience** and the **purpose** of their writing.

With friends we can be informal:

I'm really fed up!

With people we don't know so well, we might need to be more formal:

I am writing to complain about the service I have received.

FACT FILE

Animal:	Piranha
Habitat:	Amazonian rivers, South America
Weight:	Up to 3.5 kg
Lifespan:	Up to 12 years
Diet:	Other fish, insects, invertebrates and plants

Task 1

Decide whether you think each of these types of writing is likely to be formal (F) or informal (I). Write F or I in each box.

a A school report ☐

b An email to a friend ☐

c A text to your sister ☐

d A letter from the council ☐

e A newspaper report ☐

f A wedding invitation ☐

Task 2

Now look at these sentences from different types of text. Is the language formal or informal?

a Visitors to the new Piranha Pool are advised to pre-book tickets. _____

b Reduced ticket prices are available for eligible groups. _____

c The piranha tank is amazing. You're gonna love it! _____

d See you by the entrance at six-ish? _____

e Aquarium tickets are non-refundable. _____

Write these formal sentences again using informal language.

a Flash photography is forbidden in the aquarium.

_____

_____

b Please refrain from tapping on the glass, as this disturbs the fish.

_____

_____

c A range of souvenirs is available to purchase in the gift shop.

_____

_____

WILD FACT

In a feeding frenzy, a shoal of piranhas can strip the flesh from the bones of a large animal in minutes.

WILD FACT

Piranhas have powerful jaws lined with razor-sharp triangular teeth, which interlock when the mouth is closed.

Exploring Further ...

See if you can find a more formal word for each of the words in bold, hidden in the word-search grid. The first letter of each word is red to help you.

D	E	P	A	R	T	I	E	L	S
F	H	E	E	E	R	E	R	O	W
E	A	R	R	I	A	L	E	A	J
L	L	M	P	M	N	D	Q	K	M
E	C	I	K	B	F	L	U	E	P
A	K	T	C	U	O	A	E	N	E
S	U	T	T	R	L	G	S	S	A
T	N	E	O	S	D	C	T	L	L
E	E	D	K	E	E	K	E	O	D
N	O	T	I	F	I	E	D	D	M

leave

asked

told

pay back

allowed

Now swim to pages 44–45 to record what you have learned in your explorer's logbook.

Agreeable Word endings

You will discover that the word endings **ible** and **able** often sound the same when you say them. This can make spelling these words difficult. Try saying these words out loud:

forcible   *adorable*

The **able** ending is more common.

Task 1

Circle the correct word in each pair of bats.

a   credable   credible

b   adorable   adorible

c   portable   portible

d   affordable   affordible

e   visable   visible

Task 2 — Choose **ible** or **able** to complete each word.

a respons_____

b wash _____

c read _____

d poss_____

e forgiv_____

f aud _____

WILD FACT

Despite what you see in films, vampire bats are quite small and their bite is usually harmless, although they can spread disease.

Task 3 — Complete these word sums, taking care to amend the spelling of the root word where appropriate.

a achieve + able = _____

b regret + able = _____

c rely + able = _____

d deny + able = _____

e apply + able = _____

Task 4 — Read the clues then write the answers.

a Unfit to be eaten   i _____

b Can be obtained; available   o _____

c Cosy, restful, easy   c _____

d Causing great fear or alarm; awful   t _____

Exploring Further ...

Unscramble these anagrams, using the root words as a clue.

a eat   **BLEDEI**   _____

b renew   **BELAWNERE**   _____

c sense   **SSLENIEB**   _____

d permit   **LEPREMSISIB** _____

Now glide to pages 44–45 to record what you have learned in your explorer's logbook.

Vital verbs

The meaning of **verbs** can often be altered by adding a **prefix** to the beginning of the word.

overreact   _mis_behave   _re_-examine

Most prefixes can be added without changing the spelling of the root word.

FACT FILE

Animal: Bird of paradise
Habitat: Dense rainforest, mostly in New Guinea, eastern Australia and the Maluku Islands
Weight: 50 to 448 g
Lifespan: Up to 30 years
Diet: Mainly fruit and arthropods

| Task 1 | Choose the correct prefix to add to each bold word. Add a hyphen if the prefix ends with a vowel and the root word begins with one. Write the new word in the space. |

a mis   dis   over   **appear**   _____

b re   mis   dis   **able**   _____

c de   mis   dis   **activate**   _____

d over   de   dis   **heat**   _____

e un   mis   de   **calculate**   _____

Task 2
Choose a prefix to add to each of these verbs.

a _____ port

b ____connect

c ____charge

d ____estimate

e ____courage

f ____lock

g ____pick

h ____place

WILD FACT

South Africa's beautiful bird of paradise flower is named after these stunning birds because it resembles a bird of paradise in flight.

WILD FACT

Male birds of paradise are among the world's most colourful and dramatic of birds. The females are quite drab by comparison. This is so they are camouflaged while sitting on their nest.

Task 3
Circle the correct word in each group.

a disexplain   disapproach   disbelieve

b mistreat   misbelong   misdisplay

c overfall   overeat   overspeak

d dechant   dehydrate   demoan

e reclaim   regone   relimit

f unheat   unable   unsee

g misfind   misdo   misuse

h disagree   dismove   disgo

Exploring Further ...

Write your own sentences using these words.

a overactive _____

_____

b discontinue _____

_____

c overhear _____

_____

Now dart to pages 44–45 to record what you have learned in your explorer's logbook.

Super suffixes

When you add a **suffix** to a word ending in **fer**, you need to decide whether you need to double the final **r** before you add the suffix. Look at these examples:

refer   referral   reference

You must double the **r** when the **fer** is still stressed after the ending has been added.

Say the word out loud to hear whether the suffix is stressed or not.

Task 1

Circle the correctly spelt word in each pair.

a infered   inferred
b differing   differring
c conference   conference
d transferred   transfered
e sufferring   suffering

Task 2

Complete these word sums. Double the r where appropriate.

a buffer + ed   = _____

b infer + ence   = _____

c prefer + ed   = _____

d defer + ed   = _____

e proffer + ing = _____

Task 3   Draw a line to match each word with a suitable ending.

a  offer

b  confer

c  refer

d  conifer

e  pilfer

 ring

 ee

 ous

 er

 ed

WILD FACT

Leafcutter ants live together in complex colonies containing millions of ants.

WILD FACT

A leafcutter ant can carry pieces of leaf several times its own weight. These are taken back to the fungus garden to be broken down.

Exploring Further ...

Find the words in bold in the word-search grid.

F	S	E	R	F	E	R	R	E	D	B	U
E	T	R	W	C	E	D	U	T	W	U	I
R	E	E	M	N	C	N	S	F	E	F	D
P	R	E	F	E	R	E	N	C	E	F	R
S	E	F	P	B	T	N	S	F	E	E	A
U	F	E	O	U	R	T	R	A	L	R	L
F	E	R	J	F	A	B	U	F	N	I	N
T	R	A	N	S	F	E	R	R	I	N	G
A	R	N	I	R	E	F	I	N	G	G	E
R	E	T	K	E	T	K	L	O	C	E	D
E	D	I	F	F	E	R	E	D	R	A	L

preference

differed

transferring

referred

buffering

Now march to pages 44–45 to record what you have learned in your explorer's logbook.

Tricky decisions: ie or ei?

The letters **i** and **e** are often found together in words, but it can be tricky to know which order to put them in. You need to learn when to use **ie** and when to use **ei**.

_vi̲e̲w_   _ve̲i̲n_

Task 1
Choose **ie** or **ei** to complete each word.

a w___rd

b f___ld

c f___rce

d fr___nd

e h___r

f perc___ve

FACT FILE

Animal:	Sloth
Habitat:	The treetops in the rainforests of Central and South America
Weight:	Up to 10 kg
Lifespan:	10 to 40 years
Diet:	Leaves, shoots, fruits and plants

Task 2
Circle the correctly spelt word in each pair of jungle leaves.

a viel   veil

b reign   riegn

c pierce   peirce

d protien   protein

e teir   tier

f diesel   deisel

16

Task 3 Complete these sentences by unscrambling the word in bold.

a We had a wonderful **wvie** _____ of the sloths sleeping in the trees.

b I couldn't **veilbee**_____ how still they were!

c When they come down from the trees, sloths risk being **dsezie** _____ by predators.

d I was **rlieevde** _____ to see the sloth return safely to the trees.

e I dropped my hat in the forest and ran to **riveret** _____ it.

f Leaves and fruit make up part of a sloth's **edti** _____.

g The sloth came down from the tree for a **fribe** _____ moment.

Exploring Further ...

Build words by combining syllables from the box. Each syllable can be used only once; the clues will help you.

bel eipt eit rec ief ing caff ceil eine dec

a Something you think is true. _____

b Above your head in a room. _____

c A paper to prove you have paid. _____

d Found in coffee. _____

e Trickery or lies. _____

Now creep to pages 44–45 to record what you have learned in your explorer's logbook.

More word endings

Word endings **ent** and **ant** can be tricky to spell because they sound similar. Also difficult are **ence** and **ance**.

innocent   *innocence*

hesitant   *hesitance*

Exploring words with these endings will help to make you a super speller!

Task 1   Complete each word by adding **ent** or **ant**

a hesit_____

b deterg_____

c obedi_____

d toler_____

e frequ_____

f brilli_____

Task 2   Circle the correctly spelt word in each pair.

a observance   observence

b relience   reliance

c acceptence   acceptance

d excellence   excellance

e elegence   elegance

f sequence   sequance

WILD FACT

An anaconda can hunt almost fully submerged in water because its eyes and nostrils are positioned on top of its head.

WILD FACT

Anacondas are the world's heaviest snake. The females are particularly heavy, weighing up to five times as much as the males.

Task 3 Complete the table according to whether you can add **ent**, **ant**, **ence** or **ance** to each word. Take care!

		ant	ent	ance	ence
	appear	–	apparent	appearance	–
a	differ				
b	consist				
c	excel				
d	indulge				
e	apply				
f	ignore				

Exploring Further ...

Find and circle five incorrectly spelt words in the swamp.

allowance   occurance   consistent

independance   guidance

brilliant   radient   tenant

entrant   sequence

instence   gallent   reliant

persistent   excellent

Now slither to pages **44–45** to record what you
have learned in your explorer's logbook.

How Certain are you?

We often need to write about how **certain** we are about something. **Modal verbs** help us to do this:

can   might   must

We can also use **adverbs**:

possibly   surely   maybe

Choosing the right word will help us to say exactly how likely something is.

FACT FILE

Animal: Woolly monkey
Habitat: The humid tropical rainforests in the northern countries of South America
Weight: 5 to 8 kg
Lifespan: 7 to 20 years
Diet: Fruit, leaves, seeds, flowers, nuts, small insects and some small rodents and reptiles

Task 1 Underline the word in each sentence that describes how likely something is.

a At daybreak, we will head into the forest.

b We have skilled guides to help us, so we should make good progress.

c It was definitely a good idea to bring plenty of water with us.

d There must be woolly monkeys all over this part of the forest.

e We may be lucky enough to see them.

WILD FACT

Woolly monkeys have long prehensile tails, which they can use like an extra limb. They are strong enough to support the monkey's weight.

Task 2 Choose the most suitable word to complete each sentence.

a Explorers <u>ought / shall / should</u> treat the forest with respect.

b They need to be careful because they <u>may / should / must</u> encounter dangerous animals.

c They <u>should / could / would</u> be bitten by a venomous snake.

d Or <u>clearly / obviously / maybe</u> they could fall and twist their ankle.

e For these reasons, they <u>surely / should / shall</u> take a well-stocked first-aid kit with them on their expedition.

Task 3 Sort the words in the bananas into modal verbs and adverbs and add them to the table.

WILD FACT

These monkeys rarely come down to the forest floor, but when they do, they walk upright on their hind legs, a little like a person.

shall

certainly

possibly

can

obviously

would

Modal verbs	Adverbs

Exploring Further ...

Write sensible endings for these sentences.

a You could _____

b Perhaps it will _____

c I will _____

d We should all _____

Now swing to page 44–45 to record what you have learned in your explorer's logbook.

Passive verbs

We use verbs to describe actions. **Active verbs** focus on who or what is carrying out the action.

An explorer has discovered a new species of lizard.

Passive verbs focus on the person or thing the action is happening to, without mentioning who carries out the action.

A new species of lizard has been discovered.

Being able to use both active and passive verbs will improve your writing style.

WILD FACT

When threatened, the Australian frilled lizard will rear up on its hind legs, hiss and display its frill, which is 30 cm in diameter. Scary stuff!

Task 1

Decide whether each sentence uses an active or a passive verb. Write 'active' or 'passive' at the end of each sentence.

a Despite its impressive display, the lizard was forced to flee. _____

b Frilled lizards conceal themselves in trees because their skin is camouflaged. _____

c A frilled lizard will hiss in an attempt to scare potential predators. _____

d Australian frilled lizards are thought of as the national reptile of Australia. _____

Task 2 — These sentences all contain passive verbs. Underline the person or thing to which the action is happening.

a The lizard was startled and displayed its frill.

b The explorer was made famous by her discoveries.

c The insect was caught by the frilled lizard.

d Some travellers were surprised by the hissing lizard.

Task 3 — Write these active verb sentences again, using passive verbs.

a The zoologist photographed the lizard.

_____

b Frilled lizards eat insects, spiders and small reptiles.

_____

c Large snakes hunt Australian frilled lizards.

_____

d Many people keep frilled lizards as pets.

_____

Exploring Further …

Write two sentences of your own about the frilled lizard, using active and passive verbs.

_____

_____

_____

Now scuttle to pages 44–45 to record what you have learned in your explorer's logbook.

Perfect punctuation

Using punctuation will help to make your writing easier to understand.

Semi-colons can be used within sentences to mark a break that is stronger than a comma but not strong enough to need a full stop. You use them to show the link between two main clauses.

It began to rain again; the explorers sheltered in a cave.

Colons are used to introduce a list.

The explorer's emergency rations include: water, medicines, bandages and an energy bar.

WILD FACT

Armadillos can hold their breath for up to six minutes while under water or burrowing.

Task 1   **Add a semi-colon to these sentences.**

a We didn't see an armadillo I was disappointed.

b Armadillos are not good at keeping their bodies warm they live in warm places.

c Armadillos are good at digging they use burrows to escape their predators.

d An armadillo relies on its sense of smell and taste to find food it has poor eyesight.

FACT FILE

Animal: Armadillo
Habitat: Temperate, warm habitats including the rainforests in South America
Weight: 85 g to 54 kg
Lifespan: Up to 15 years
Diet: Insects including termites, ants and beetles

| Task 2 | Add a colon to these sentences. |

a When exploring in a hot climate you should take the following a hat, sunscreen, insect repellent and plenty of water.

b The explorer's notebook has sections for the following animals birds, insects, mammals and reptiles.

c There are rainforests in the following places South and Central America, Africa, Oceania and Asia.

d Many of the things we take for granted come from the rainforest spices, medicines, rubber and pineapples.

WILD FACT

The name armadillo means 'little armoured one' in Spanish. They are the only mammals to have a tough armour-like shell.

| Task 3 | Add a colon or semi-colon to each of these sentences. |

a Many areas of rainforest are threatened we should work to protect them.

b Rainforests are thought to be home to many undiscovered species of the following plants, insects and microorganisms.

c The explorers looked out for the following venomous animals snakes, spiders and scorpions.

d Many undiscovered species live in rainforests there is still a lot to explore.

Exploring Further ...

Circle a mistake in each of these sentences. Then write the correct sentence below.

a Rainforest creatures feed on the following parts of; plants, leaves, flowers, fruit and seeds.

_____

_____

b The explorer became very famous she discovered a new species: of butterfly.

_____

_____

Now dig to pages 44–45 to record what you have learned in your explorer's logbook.

Building verbs

You can use **suffixes** to changes nouns and adjectives into **verbs**.

intense + ify = intensify

replica + ate = replicate

You often need to alter the spelling of the **root word** before you add the suffix.

Task 1 Complete the word sums to make verbs.

a captive + ate = _____

b real + ise = _____

c weak + en = _____

d false + ify = _____

FACT FILE

Animal: Toucan
Habitat: The tropical rainforests of South America
Weight: 550 g
Lifespan: Up to 20 years
Diet: Mainly fruit

Task 2 Choose a suffix from a flower to add to each word (you may use them more than once). Write the new word in the space provided.

ate   ify   ise   en

a public _____   d ripe _____

b formula _____   e sign _____

c fantasy _____   f replica _____

Task 3 Circle the correct word in each group.

a lenthify   lengthate   lengthen

b intensate   intensify   intensise

c specialise   specialify   specialate

d validise   validify   validate

e medicise   medicate   medicify

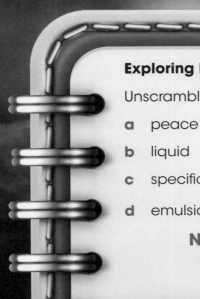

Task 4 Combine a noun with a suffix to complete each of these sentences.

Nouns:	priority	length	class	Suffixes:	en	ify	ise

a I would not _____ the toucan as an endangered bird.

b We should _____ seeing some toucans today.

c The baby toucan's beak will _____ as it grows.

Exploring Further ...

Unscramble the verbs made from these words.

a peace   **CYPAFI**   _____

b liquid   **YQFUILE**   _____

c specific   **YSPIECF**   _____

d emulsion   **LUYEFMIS**   _____

Now fly to pages 44–45 to record what you have learned in your explorer's logbook.

Hyphens

Hyphens are useful punctuation marks that we can use to make our writing clearer.

bird eating spider
bird-eating spider ← Just who is eating whom here?

We can use **hyphens** to show more about how words are related to each other.

We can also use hyphens when adding **prefixes**, to aid clarity or to avoid clumsy double vowels.

cooperate   *co-operate*
coauthor   *co-author*

FACT FILE

Animal: Goliath bird-eating spider
Habitat: Wet swamps, marshy areas and rainforests of South America
Weight: Up to 170 g
Lifespan: 3 to 25 years
Diet: Occasionally hatchling birds but mainly insects lizards, frogs and other spiders

Task 1 Write these words again, adding a hyphen after the prefix.

a reapply _____

b coordinate _____

c reinvent _____

d coown _____

e reenrol _____

f reissue _____

WILD FACT

These spiders can defend themselves by launching fine hairs at their foe, causing extreme irritation to the skin, eyes and nose.

Task 2 Join each word to the correct definition, using the hyphens to help you.

a re-cover   form again

b recover   amend and improve

c re-form   get over an illness or injury

d reform   cover again

Task 3 Examine these sentences. In each one, what does the hyphen suggest has been lost? Tick the correct word.

a The explorer returned the lost-baggage form to the airport.

baggage ☐   form ☐

b The explorer returned the lost baggage-form to the airport.

baggage ☐   form ☐

In these sentences, how often did the scientist submit her reports?

c The scientist submitted three-monthly reports of her findings.

every month ☐   every three months ☐

d The scientist submitted three monthly reports of her findings.

every month ☐   every three months ☐

Exploring Further ...

Choose the most suitable option to complete each sentence.

a The guide remarked / re-marked that the weather looked fine.

b I had to re-sign / resign the letter after the ink ran in the rain.

c I re-dressed / redressed the spider bite to keep it clean.

d I resent / re-sent the email with the new attachment.

Now spin to pages 44–45 to record what you have learned in your explorer's logbook.

Endings: cial or tial?

Words ending **cial** and **tial** sound very similar when they are pronounced, so we need to learn when to use each one.

cial often follows a vowel:

super<u>ficial</u>

tial often follows a consonant:

confiden<u>tial</u>

However, you will discover that there are exceptions that you need to watch out for!

Task 1

Circle the correctly spelt word in each pair.

a commertial   commercial

b essential   essencial

c special   spetial

d potential   potencial

e residencial   residential

Task 2

Add **cial** or **tial** to complete each word.

a finan_____

b presiden_____

c ini_____

d cru_____

e offi_____

f gla_____

WILD FACT

The habitat of these endangered butterflies is being lost as palm-oil, cocoa and rubber plantations expand.

Task 3 — Complete these word sums, taking care with spelling.

a palace + ial = _____

b artifice + ial = _____

c influence + ial = _____

d sacrifice + ial = _____

e face + ial = _____

Task 4 — Choose a word from the box and add an appropriate **cial** or **tial** suffix. Use one word in each of these sentences.

> office   benefit   torrent   substance

a The butterflies shelter under leaves from the _____ rain.

b The poisonous vines are _____ to the birdwing butterfly.

c The danger of losing the birdwing butterfly due to agricultural expansion is _____.

d It's _____: the Queen Alexandra's birdwing butterfly is the biggest in the world!

Exploring Further ...

Find the words in bold in the word-search grid.

E	R	S	A	P	E	A	R	F	F	I
P	R	O	V	I	N	C	I	A	L	O
T	O	C	R	A	C	I	E	C	A	L
O	V	I	M	P	A	R	T	I	A	L
C	I	A	R	T	P	C	A	A	R	T
I	N	L	C	I	L	I	A	L	E	D
A	C	R	E	D	E	N	T	I	A	L

provincial

impartial

facial

social

credential

Now flutter to pages 44–45 to record what you have learned in your explorer's logbook.

Fact and opinion

You can discover all sorts of wonderful things by reading! Being able to tell the difference between **facts** and **opinions** will help you to form your own views about what you read.

Facts can be proven to be **true**.

More than half of the world's plants and animals live in rainforests.

Opinions are the **personal views** of an individual.

I think rainforests should be protected.

Task 1 — Decide whether each of these sentences is likely to be a fact or an opinion. Write 'fact' or 'opinion' at the end of each sentence.

a An elephant's tusk can reach 150 cm long. _____

b Elephants are the world's largest land-dwelling mammal. _____

c People should not buy items made from ivory. _____

d We need to make sure that elephants are protected. _____

WILD FACT

Elephants can communicate with each other across long distances with a rumbling sound so low that humans can't hear it.

FACT FILE

Animal: African forest elephant
Habitat: The tropical forests of the equatorial west and Central Africa
Weight: 2700 kg
Lifespan: 60 to 70 years
Diet: Leaves, fruit and bark

Task 2 Examine this piece of text about African forest elephants. Circle three facts and underline two opinions in the text.

Elephants are beautiful animals but they are often hunted for their tusks, which are made of ivory. The tusk of an African forest elephant can weigh as much as a small human adult. Elephants must be much happier in zoos.

Task 3 Write three sentences about your opinion of African forest elephants. Remember, your opinions are all about what YOU think.

a _____

_____

b _____

_____

c _____

_____

WILD FACT

African forest elephants have straighter tusks than African bush elephants, to help them move easily through the trees.

WILD FACT

An African forest elephant can drink up to 220 litres of water each day.

Exploring Further ...

There are many more facts to discover about African forest elephants. Can you write down three questions that you could ask to find out more facts about these animals?

a _____

b _____

c _____

Now charge to pages 44–45 to record what you have learned in your explorer's logbook.

The *ough* letter string

As you explore the English language, you will discover that the **ough** letter string can be used to spell several different sounds.

through   *cough*   *ought*

Investigating this letter string will help you to tackle the spelling of more difficult words.

Task 1

Draw lines to match up pairs of words in which **ough** makes the same sound.

a bought   enough

b tough   though

c dough   bough

d thorough   borough

e plough   fought

WILD FACT

Macaws are very social birds and they often gather in large flocks. Macaws use squawks, screams and calls to communicate with each other, to mark their territory and to identify one another. Some species can even mimic human speech.

WILD FACT

You might think that the colourful feathers of the macaw would make them stand out to predators, but they actually blend right in amongst the shards of sunlight in the forest canopy.

FACT FILE

Animal: Macaw
Habitat: Rainforests, forest grasslands and riverside forests in Mexico and Central and South America
Weight: 129 to 1659 g
Lifespan: Up to 60 years
Diet: Fruits, nuts, seeds, leaves, flowers

Task 2 Choose the correct word to complete each sentence.

a Macaws have a <u>ruff / rough</u> tongue to help them to manipulate the nuts they eat.

b Their beautiful feathers make them <u>sought / sort</u> after as pets.

c They are able to hide in the glints of light shining <u>threw / through</u> the trees.

d Macaws have specially adapted claws for gripping the <u>boughs / bows</u> of trees.

Task 3 Each of the words on the leaves rhymes with a word below. Can you match them up?

buffed **port** **cow** **scoff** **blue** **know**

a trough _____

b dough _____

c wrought _____

d through _____

e plough _____

f roughed _____

WILD FACT

The hyacinth macaw is the largest of all parrots. Its wingspan is over 1.2 metres.

Exploring Further ...

You will find that the **ough** letter string often appears in past tense verbs. See if you can complete this table.

Present tense	Past tense
bring	
seek	
think	
buy	
fight	

Now squawk to pages 44–45 to record what you have learned in your explorer's logbook.

Clever clauses

When we want to add extra information to our writing but don't want to start a new sentence, we can use a **relative clause**.

She is the famous explorer <u>who wrote about tarsiers</u>.

The book <u>that she wrote</u> has just been published.

Relative clauses often start with **who**, **which**, **where**, **when**, **whose** or **that**. If you remove them from the sentence, what is left will still make sense.

FACT FILE

Animal:	Tarsier
Habitat:	Well-vegetated forests in a few islands in Malaysia, Indonesia and the southern Philippines
Weight:	80 g to 165 g
Lifespan:	12 to 20 years
Diet:	Insects, birds, crabs, snakes and bats

Task 1   Underline the relative clause in each sentence.

a   We were in this rainforest when we first saw tarsiers.

b   The zoologist made a discovery which changed our understanding of the rainforest.

c   The drawings that I made showed the forest canopy.

d   The tarsiers, whose eyes were very bright, looked right at us.

Task 2

Circle the most appropriate word from the choices given to complete each sentence.

a The explorers were climbing the mountain <u>when / where</u> night fell.

b Tarsiers are small primates <u>when / whose</u> long legs enable them to leap.

c We found the clearing <u>where / when</u> the tarsiers live.

d We didn't see any tarsiers <u>when / where</u> our expedition arrived.

e These are the tarsiers <u>whose / where</u> habitat is under threat.

f This is an island <u>when / where</u> the tarsiers live.

Task 3

Add a suitable word to complete these sentences.

a Here is the cave _____ we sheltered.

b Those are the birds _____ sing at night.

c Here are the books _____ describe tarsiers.

d There is the forest _____ the tarsiers live.

e These are the insects _____ the tarsiers eat.

WILD FACT

A tarsier can rotate its head 180 degrees in either direction, allowing it to look behind itself without moving its body.

Exploring Further ...

Finish these sentences by completing the relative clause.

a This is the path that _____

_____

b They pitched their tents when _____

_____

c We crossed the river where _____

_____

Now leap to pages 44–45 to record what you have learned in your explorer's logbook.

Synonyms and antonyms

Synonyms are words with **similar** meanings. They help us to add variety to our writing and avoid repeating the same word again.

exploration   expedition

Antonyms are words with **opposite** meanings. They are useful for comparing and contrasting things.

ascend   descend

FACT FILE

Animal: Bengal tiger
Habitat: Tropical rainforests and mangroves in southern and south-eastern Asia
Weight: 109 to 227 kg
Lifespan: 8 to 10 years
Diet: Birds, monkeys, wild pigs, boars, wolves and antelope

Task 1   Sort these words into groups of synonyms and put them together into the paws.

jungle   journey   discover   find   forest   trip   tour   wood   locate

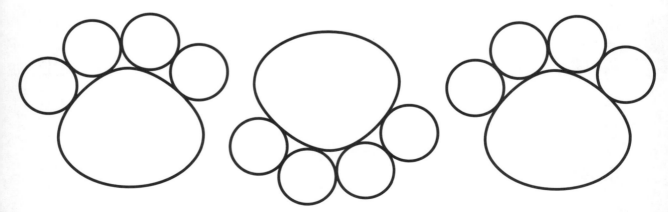

Task 2

Synonyms rarely have exactly the same meaning. Choose the most appropriate synonym to complete each sentence.

a The explorer <u>pursued / followed / chased</u> the track into the forest.

b Everyone knows that tigers are <u>treacherous / perilous / dangerous</u> animals.

c The explorer was <u>alert / perceptive / sharp</u> for sounds of danger hidden in the trees.

d He was ready to <u>depart / flee / desert</u> at any moment.

e Up ahead, a break in the undergrowth <u>revealed / declared / divulged</u> a glimpse of a tiger.

WILD FACT

A tiger's stripes are like a fingerprint; each tiger has a unique pattern of stripes.

Task 3

Now draw lines to match each word with an antonym.

a narrow	criticise
b occupied	innocent
c praise	broad
d guilty	precede
e follow	vacant

WILD FACT

Unusually for members of the cat family, tigers enjoy being in the water and are strong swimmers. They like to live near water.

Exploring Further ...

Write a synonym and antonym for each of these words.

		synonym	antonym
a	**expand**		
b	**foolish**		
c	**brave**		
d	**repair**		

Now pad to pages 44–45 to record what you have learned in your explorer's logbook.

Proofreading

No matter how careful you are with your writing, it is easy to make mistakes. **Proofreading** your writing when you have finished will help you to **spot errors** and finds ways to improve your work.

Watt a sensable idear!

Task 1 Underline a spelling mistake in each sentence. Write the correctly spelt word on the line below.

a The explorer was contious of being watched by something in the trees.

_____

b It was possable to see chimpanzees resting in the branches.

_____

c You need patiance to watch these amazing animals.

_____

d We espetially enjoyed watching the chimpanzees feeding.

_____

e They polked long sticks into the bees nest to reach the honey.

_____

FACT FILE

Animal: Chimpanzee
Habitat: African rainforests, woodlands, and grasslands
Weight: 30 to 60 kg
Lifespan: Up to 50 years
Diet: Fruits, seeds, nuts, leaves, flowers, insects and medium-sized mammals.

Task 2   Correct the punctuation in each sentence.

a   We watched the chimpanzees use the following tools; sticks stones and leaves.

b   "That is so clever! exclaimed" the zoologist.

c   Chimanzees coop-erate to gather food for the troop.

d   Many people are fascinated by chimpanzees. they are so like us.

Task 3   This writer has made a mistake with a homophone in each sentence. Locate and underline the mistake, then write the correct word at the end.

a   We watched a young chimpanzee steel some fruit from her brother. _____

b   The farther of the chimpanzee took the fruit back. _____

c   The young chimpanzee let out a grown of frustration. _____

d   By early mourning, most of the chimpanzees were sleeping in the trees. _____

e   Hardly a sound could be herd. _____

Exploring Further …

Write this piece of text again, correcting any mistakes you find.

The chimpanzee broke the stick into peices and used them to scoop honey from the nest. The sticky honey was obviously delectible. He offered to share the honey with the chimpanzee next to him. This young chimpanzee was a little hesitent to come forward, as the angry bees buzzed around them.

_____

_____

_____

_____

_____

Now swing to pages 44–45 to record what you have learned in your explorer's logbook.

Quick test

Now try these questions. Give yourself 1 mark for every correct answer – but only if you answer each part of the question correctly.

1 Identify the silent letter missing from these words:

reck   sord   anser   _____

2 Add a or e to complete the bold word in this sentence:

The weather may __**ffect** our expedition.

3 Circle the correctly spelt word to complete the sentence:

Explorers visiting the rainforest must beware of infecious / infectious diseases.

4 Are these features more likely to be found in formal or informal writing? Tick the box to indicate your answer.

slang   formal   ☐   informal   ☐

abbreviations   formal   ☐   informal   ☐

emoticons   formal   ☐   informal   ☐

5 Circle the correctly spelt word in this pair:

terrable   terrible

6 Circle the correct word in this group:

overcover   disembark   reguided   misfollow

7 Complete this word sum:

confer + ing = _____

8 Unscramble the anagram to reveal a word containing a silent letter which means 'from another country':

GIFERON   _____

9 Either e or a will complete all of these words. Decide which letter you think it is and add it to the words:

domin__nt   vari_nce   clear_nce

10 Sort these words into the table to show how certain something is:

could   definitely   possibly   must

may happen	will happen

11 Does this sentence have an active or passive verb?

The rare bird was tracked through the forest by the zoologist.

active ☐   passive ☐

12 Add either a colon or a semi-colon in the space indicated in this sentence:

Young explorers can discover more about animals in the following places ___ libraries, museums, bookshops and schools.

13 Complete the word sum:

priority + ise = _____

14 Write your own sentences using these words:

re-present _____

_____

represent _____

_____

15 Circle the correctly spelt word:

circumstancial   circumstantial

16 Write 'fact' or 'opinion' at the end of these definitions:

Information that can be proved.   _____

The views of an individual.   _____

17 Write down any word which rhymes with the sound of the ough letter string in this word:

nought   _____

18 Underline the relative clause in this sentence:

This is the bird which made that nest.

19 Circle the word which is not a synonym of receive:

obtain   accept   gain   forfeit   collect

20 Underline a spelling mistake in this sentence:

It is essencial to travel with the proper equipment.

How did you do?   **1–5 Try again**   **6–10 Good try!**

11–15 Great work!   **16–20 Excellent exploring!**

/20

Explorer's Logbook

Tick off the topics as you complete them and then colour in the star.

More word endings ☐

Clever clauses ☐

Endings: cial or tial? ☐

Building verbs ☐

Formal or informal? ☐

Agreeable word endings ☐

Fact and opinion ☐

The ough letter string ☐

Passive verbs ☐

Super suffixes ☐

Shh . . . silent letters! ☐

Proofreading ☐

Hyphens ☐

Homophones ☐

Tricky word endings ☐

Synonyms and antonyms ☐

How certain are you? ☐

Tricky decisions: ie or ei? ☐

Perfect punctuation ☐

Vital verbs ☐

Answers

Pages 2-3
Task 1
a chalk **b** limb **c** gnome **d** knee
e island **f** raspberry **g** dumb **h** whistle
i comb **j** knock **k** thumb **l** write
m knit **n** sign **o** crumb **p** wrist
Task 2
Possible answers include:
a wrinkle, wrap **b** limb, comb **c** science, scene
d chalk, stalk **e** sign, design **f** ghost, ghoul
Task 3
a sine/sign **b** now/know
c gard/guard **d** dout/doubt
Exploring Further
a AUTUMN **b** CALM
c KNEE **d** THISTLE

Pages 4-5
Task 1
a desert **b** dessert **c** allowed
d aloud **e** deer **f** dear
Task 2
a assent **b** mourning
c who's **d** Their
Task 3
a recent **b** led **c** stationary **d** proceed
Exploring Further
Any sentence is acceptable which uses the given word in the correct context and is grammatically correct.

Pages 6-7
Task 1
a spacious **b** gracious **c** nutritious
d vicious **e** facetious **f** facetious
Task 2
a precious **b** cautious **c** ambitious **d** delicious
e fictitious **f** luscious **g** conscious
Task 3
a vivacious = lively, energetic
b malicious = spiteful or intended to harm
c scrumptious = really tasty
d tenacious = determined
e repetitious = tiresomely repetitive
Exploring Further
a suspicious **b** ferocious **c** ostentatious
d luscious **e** contentious **f** atrocious

Pages 8-9
Task 1
a Formal **b** Informal **c** Informal
d Formal **e** Formal **f** Formal
Task 2
a Formal **b** Formal **c** Informal
d Informal **e** Formal
Task 3
Possible answers include:
a You can't use flash photography in the aquarium.
b Please don't tap on the glass because it disturbs the fish.
c You can buy souvenirs in the gift shop.
Exploring Further

D	E	P	A	R	T	I	E	L	S
F	H	E	E	E	R	E	R	O	W
E	A	R	R	I	A	L	E	A	J
L	L	M	P	M	N	D	Q	K	M
E	C	I	K	B	F	L	U	E	P
A	K	T	C	U	O	A	E	N	E
S	U	T	T	R	L	G	S	S	A
T	N	E	O	S	D	C	T	L	L
E	E	D	K	E	E	K	E	O	D
N	O	T	I	F	I	E	D	D	M

Pages 10-11
Task 1
a credible **b** adorable **c** portable
d affordable **e** visible
Task 2
a responsible **b** washable **c** readable
d possible **e** forgivable **f** audible
Task 3
a achievable **b** regrettable **c** reliable
d deniable **e** applicable
Task 4
a inedible **b** obtainable
c comfortable **d** terrible
Exploring Further
a EDIBLE **b** RENEWABLE
c SENSIBLE **d** PERMISSIBLE

Pages 12-13
Task 1
a disappear **b** disable **c** de-activate
d overheat **e** miscalculate
Task 2
Various answers are possible. Examples include:
a deport, report
b disconnect, reconnect
c recharge, overcharge
d overestimate, underestimate
e discourage, encourage
f unlock, relock
g unpick, mispick
h misplace, replace
Task 3
a disbelieve **b** mistreat **c** overeat **d** dehydrate
e reclaim **f** unable **g** misuse **h** disagree
Exploring Further
Any sentences are acceptable which use the given word in an appropriate context.

Pages 14-15
Task 1
a inferred **b** differing **c** conference
d transferred **e** suffering
Task 2
a buffered **b** inference **c** preferred
d deferred **e** proffering
Task 3
a offered **b** conferring **c** referee
d coniferous **e** pilferer
Exploring Further

F	S	E	R	F	E	R	R	E	D	B	U
E	T	R	W	C	E	D	U	T	W	U	I
R	E	E	M	N	C	N	S	F	E	F	D
P	R	E	F	E	R	E	N	C	E	F	R
S	E	F	P	B	T	N	S	F	E	E	A
U	F	E	O	U	R	T	R	A	L	R	L
F	E	R	J	F	A	B	U	F	N	I	N
T	R	A	N	S	F	E	R	R	I	N	G
A	R	N	I	R	E	F	I	N	G	G	E
R	E	T	K	E	T	K	L	O	C	E	D
E	D	I	F	F	E	R	E	D	R	A	L

Pages 16-17
Task 1
a weird **b** field **c** fierce **d** friend **e** heir **f** perceive
Task 2
a veil **b** reign **c** pierce
d protein **e** tier **f** diesel
Task 3
a view **b** believe **c** seized **d** relieved
e retrieve **f** diet **g** brief

Exploring Further
a belief   **b** ceiling   **c** receipt
d caffeine   **e** deceit

Pages 18–19
Task 1
a hesitant   **b** detergent   **c** obedient
d tolerant   **e** frequent   **f** brilliant
Task 2
a observance   **b** reliance   **c** acceptance
d excellence   **e** elegance   **f** sequence
Task 3
a differ: different difference
b consist: consistent consistence
c excel: excellent excellence
d indulge: indulgent indulgence
e apply: applicant: appliance
f ignore: ignorant ignorance

Exploring Further
Incorrect words are: occurance, independance, radient, gallent, instence

Pages 20–21
Task 1
a will   **b** should   **c** definitely
d must   **e** may
Task 2
a should   **b** may   **c** could
d maybe   **e** should
Task 3

Modal verbs	Adverbs
shall	certainly
can	possibly
would	obviously

Exploring Further
Any sentence is acceptable which responds appropriately to the given verb or adverb and is grammatically correct.

Pages 22–23
Task 1
a Passive   **b** Active
c Active   **d** Passive
Task 2
a lizard   **b** explorer
c insect   **d** travellers
Task 3
a The lizard was photographed by the zoologist.
b Insects, spiders and small reptiles are eaten by frilled lizards.
c Australian frilled lizards are hunted by large snakes.
d Frilled lizards are kept as pets by many people.

Exploring Further
Any sentences which correctly use active and passive verbs are acceptable.

Pages 24–25
Task 1
a We didn't see an armadillo; I was disappointed.
b Armadillos are not good at keeping their bodies warm; they live in warm places.
c Armadillos are good at digging; they use burrows to escape their predators.
d An armadillo relies on its sense of smell and taste to find food; it has poor eyesight.
Task 2
a When exploring in a hot climate you should take the following: a hat, sunscreen, insect repellent and plenty of water.
b The explorer's notebook has sections for the following animals: birds, insects, mammals and reptiles.
c There are rainforests in the following places: South and Central America, Africa, Oceania and Asia.
d Many of the things we take for granted come from the rainforest: spices, medicines, rubber and pineapples.
Task 3
a Many areas of rainforest are threatened; we should work to protect them.

b Rainforests are thought to be home to many undiscovered species of the following: plants, insects and microorganisms.
c The explorers looked out for the following venomous animals: snakes, spiders and scorpions.
d Many undiscovered species live in rainforests; there is still a lot to explore.
Exploring Further
a Rainforest creatures feed on the following parts of plants: leaves, flowers, fruit and seeds.
b The explorer became very famous; she discovered a new species of butterfly.

Pages 26–27
Task 1
a captivate   **b** realise   **c** weaken
d falsify
Task 2
a publicise   **b** formulate   **c** fantasise
d ripen   **e** signify   **f** replicate
Task 3
a lengthen   **b** intensify   **c** specialise
d validate   **e** medicate
Task 4
a classify   **b** prioritise   **c** lengthen
Exploring Further
a PACIFY   **b** LIQUIFY   **c** SPECIFY   **d** EMULSIFY

Pages 28–29
Task 1
a re-apply   **b** co-ordinate   **c** re-invent
d co-own   **e** re-enrol   **f** re-issue
Task 2
a re-cover – cover again
b recover – get over an illness or injury
c re-form – form again
d reform – amend and improve
Task 3
a baggage   **b** form
c every three months   **d** every month
Exploring Further
a remarked   **b** re-sign
c re-dressed   **d** re-sent

Pages 30–31
Task 1
a commercial   **b** essential   **c** special
d potential   **e** residential
Task 2
a financial   **b** presidential   **c** initial
d crucial   **e** official   **f** glacial
Task 3
a palatial   **b** artificial   **c** influential   **d** sacrificial   **e** facial
Task 4
a torrential   **b** beneficial   **c** substantial   **d** official
Exploring Further

E	R	S	A	P	E	A	R	F	F	I
P	R	O	V	I	N	C	I	A	L	O
T	O	C	R	A	C	I	E	C	A	L
O	V	I	M	P	A	R	T	I	A	L
C	I	A	R	T	P	C	A	A	R	T
I	N	L	C	I	L	I	A	L	E	D
A	C	R	E	D	E	N	T	I	A	L

Pages 32–33
Task 1
Facts: **a**, **b**   Opinions: **c**, **d**
Task 2
Facts: 1) they are often hunted for their tusks, 2) tusks, which are made of ivory. 3) The tusk of an African forest elephant can weigh as much as a small human adult.
Opinions: 1) Elephants are beautiful animals. 2) Elephants must be much happier in zoos.
Task 3
Any sentences are acceptable which explain sensible personal opinions about elephants and are grammatically correct.
Exploring Further
Any questions are acceptable which might elicit factual information about elephants.

Pages 34–35
Task 1
a bought, fought **b** tough, enough **c** dough, though
d thorough, borough **e** plough, bough
Task 2
a rough **b** sought
c through **d** boughs
Task 3
a trough, scoff **b** dough, know **c** wrought, port
d through, blue **e** plough, cow **f** roughed, buffed
Exploring Further

Present tense	Past tense
bring	brought
seek	sought
think	thought
buy	bought
fight	fought

Pages 36–37
Task 1
a We were in this rainforest <u>when we first saw tarsiers</u>.
b The zoologist made a discovery <u>which changed our understanding of the rainforest</u>.
c The drawings <u>that I made</u> showed the forest canopy.
d The tarsiers, <u>whose eyes were very bright</u>, looked right at us.
Task 2
a when **b** whose **c** where
d when **e** whose **f** where
Task 3
a where **b** that or which **c** which or that
d where **e** that or which
Exploring Further
Any sentences are acceptable which have added a relative subordinate clause to the given clause.

Pages 38–39
Task 1

jungle	tour	locate
forest	journey	discover
wood	trip	find

Task 2
a followed **b** dangerous **c** alert
d flee **e** revealed
Task 3
a narrow, broad **b** occupied, vacant **c** praise, criticise
d guilty, innocent **e** follow, precede
Exploring Further
Possible answers include:

		synonym	antonym
a	expand	grow	contract
b	foolish	silly	wise
c	brave	heroic	cowardly
d	repair	mend	damage

Pages 40–41
a The explorer was <u>contious</u> of being watched by something in the trees.   conscious
b It was <u>possable</u> to see chimpanzees resting in the branches.   possible
c You need <u>patiance</u> to watch these amazing animals.   patience
d We <u>espetially</u> enjoyed watching the chimpanzees feeding.   especially
e They <u>polked</u> long sticks into the bees nest to reach the honey.   poked
Task 2
a We watched the chimpanzees use the following tools: sticks stones and leaves.
b "That is so clever!" exclaimed the zoologist.
c Chimanzees co-operate to gather food for the troop.
d Many people are fascinated by chimpanzees; they are so like us.

Task 3
a We watched a young chimpanzee <u>steel</u> some fruit from its brother.   steal
b The <u>farther</u> of the chimpanzee took the fruit back.   father
c The young chimpanzee let out a <u>grown</u> of fustration.   groan
d By early <u>mourning</u> most of the chimpanzees were sleeping in the trees.   morning
e Hardly a sound could be <u>herd</u>.   heard
Exploring Further
The chimpanzee broke the stick into <u>pieces</u> and used them to scoop honey from the nest. The sticky honey was obviously <u>delectable</u>. He offered to share the honey with the chimpanzee next to him. This young chimpanzee was a little <u>hesitant</u> to come forward, as the angry bees buzzed around them.

Answers to quick test
1 wreck, sword, answer
2 The weather may affect our expedition.
3 Explorers visiting the rainforest must beware of infectious diseases.
4 Informal, informal, informal
5 terrible
6 disembark
7 conferring
8 FOREIGN
9 dominant, variance, clearance
10

may happen	will happen
could	definitely
possibly	must

11 Passive
12 Young explorers can discover more about animals in the following places: libraries, museums, bookshops and schools.
13 prioritise
14 Answers will vary. Possible sentences include:
  I had to re-present my new findings.
  He will represent the scientists at the conference.
15 circumstantial
16 Information which can be proved = fact. The views of an individual = opinion.
17 Answers will vary. Possible answers include: paw, flaw, taut.
18 This is the bird <u>which made that nest</u>.
19 forfeit
20 It is <u>essencial</u> to travel with the proper equipment.